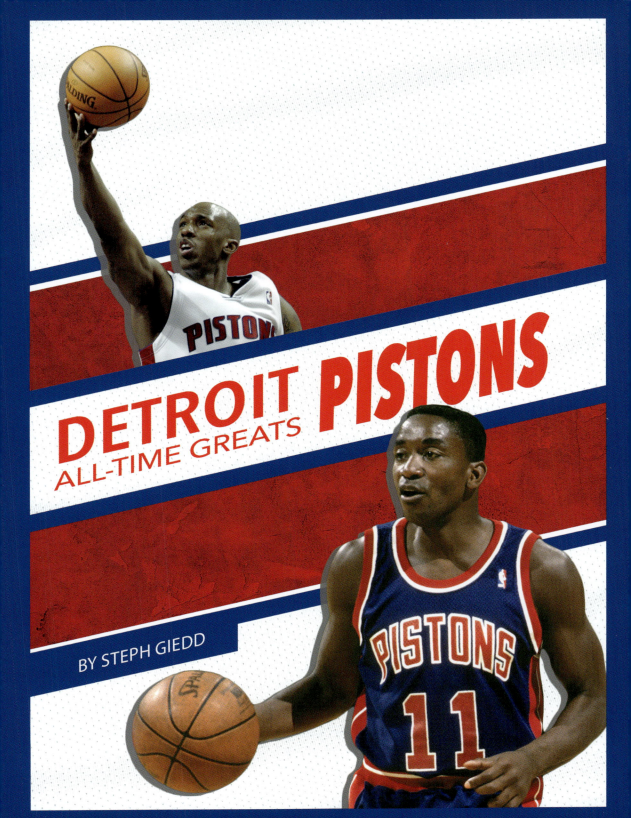

DETROIT PISTONS
ALL-TIME GREATS

BY STEPH GIEDD

Copyright © 2024 by Press Room Editions. All rights reserved. No part of this book may be used or reproduced in any manner whatsoever, including internet usage, without written permission from the copyright owner, except in the case of brief quotations embodied in critical articles and reviews.

Book design by Jake Slavik
Cover design by Jake Slavik

Photographs ©: Carlos Osorio/AP Images, cover (top), 1 (top); Al Messerschmidt Archive/Messa/AP Images, cover (bottom), 1 (bottom); AP Images, 4; FHJ/AP Images, 6; WGI/AP Images, 8; Craig Fuji/AP Images, 10; Lennox McLendon/AP Images, 13; Al Messerschmidt Archive/Messa/AP Images, 14; Duane Burleson/AP Images, 16; Michael Conroy/AP Images, 19; Paul Sancya/AP Images, 20

Press Box Books, an imprint of Press Room Editions.

ISBN
978-1-63494-661-2 (library bound)
978-1-63494-685-8 (paperback)
978-1-63494-732-9 (epub)
978-1-63494-709-1 (hosted ebook)

Library of Congress Control Number: 2022919959

Distributed by North Star Editions, Inc.
2297 Waters Drive
Mendota Heights, MN 55120
www.northstareditions.com

Printed in the United States of America
Mankato, MN
082023

ABOUT THE AUTHOR

Steph Giedd is a former high school English teacher turned sports editor. Originally from southern Iowa, Steph now lives in Minneapolis with her husband, daughter, and pets.

TABLE OF CONTENTS

CHAPTER 1
REVVING UP 4

CHAPTER 2
THE BAD BOYS 10

CHAPTER 3
DETROIT DEFENSE 16

TIMELINE 22
TEAM FACTS 23
MORE INFORMATION 23
GLOSSARY 24
INDEX 24

CHAPTER 1
REVVING UP

The Detroit Pistons have always been known for their tough style of play. That toughness didn't begin in Detroit, though. The Pistons got their start in 1941 in Fort Wayne, Indiana.

One of the best players in the Pistons' early days was 6'9" center **Larry Foust**. He joined the team in 1950. Foust was known for his strong rebounding. The big man grabbed 10.9 per game in seven seasons with the Pistons.

Small forward **George Yardley** joined the Pistons in the 1953–54 season. Yardley's talent was getting to the paint and the free throw line.

That's how he scored 2,001 points in 1957–58. That was the first time in NBA history a player had scored 2,000 points in a season. Foust and Yardley led the Pistons to the NBA Finals in 1955 and 1956. But they fell short in both years.

Forward **Dave DeBusschere** started playing in Detroit in 1962–63. In 1964–65, he started coaching the team, too. DeBusschere made two All-Star teams while he was a player-coach. **Dave Bing** was the 1966–67 Rookie of the Year. The speedy point guard made the Pistons offense run. Bing led the team in assists every year he

MOTOR CITY

Pistons owner Frank Zollner chose to move the team from Fort Wayne in 1957. He wanted to go to a bigger city. Because of Detroit's successful car industry, Zollner decided to keep the name Pistons. A piston is a car part.

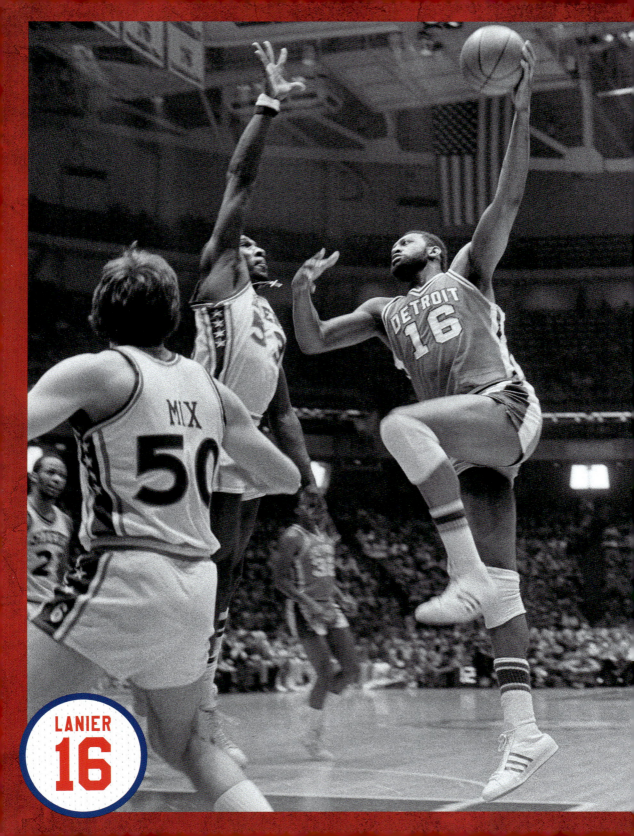

played for Detroit. He was a great scorer, too. Bing averaged more than 22 points per game with the Pistons.

In 1970, Detroit earned the first pick in the draft. The team chose 6'11" center **Bob Lanier**. He replaced Bing as the Pistons' main scorer. Lanier led the team in scoring for seven seasons.

Bing and Lanier are both enshrined in the Hall of Fame. But they never had much success in the playoffs with Detroit.

STAT SPOTLIGHT

CAREER POINTS PER GAME
PISTONS TEAM RECORD
Bob Lanier: 22.7

CHAPTER 2
THE BAD BOYS

The Pistons started to have more success in the 1980s. Drafting point guard **Isiah Thomas** in 1981 was a big reason why. Thomas was only 6'1". He was known for his toughness, though. Thomas dazzled fans with his crafty ways of getting to the rim. And he loved to share the ball with his teammates. "Zeke" led the league with 13.9 assists per

STAT SPOTLIGHT

CAREER ASSISTS
PISTONS TEAM RECORD
Isiah Thomas: 9,061

game in 1984–85. That was the highest average in a season in NBA history at the time.

Shooting guard **Vinnie Johnson** played alongside Thomas. Johnson could heat up quickly off the bench. That's why he was called the "Microwave." The Pistons drafted another talented guard in 1985 to play with Thomas. **Joe Dumars** was a nightmare for opposing guards. He made the All-Defensive Team five times.

Like Johnson, center **Bill Laimbeer** came to the Pistons in 1982. Standing at 6'11", he was a force under the hoop. Laimbeer was a great rebounder. And he was an enforcer for his teammates. Big man **Rick Mahorn** anchored the tough frontcourt in Detroit. An opposing broadcaster once called Laimbeer and Mahorn "McFilthy and McNasty." That was because

of their physical play. The toughness of this era in Detroit earned them the nickname the "Bad Boys."

Adding to Detroit's toughness was forward **Dennis Rodman**. "The Worm" could defend anyone on the court. Rodman won the league's Defensive Player of the Year Award in both 1990 and 1991.

The Pistons lost in the NBA Finals in 1988. They traded for small forward **Mark Aguirre** during the 1988–89 season. His scoring helped complete a championship roster. Detroit went on to win the Finals in 1989 and 1990.

DREAM TEAM

Hall of Fame coach Chuck Daly led the Pistons for nine seasons before becoming the coach of the 1992 U.S. Olympic men's basketball team. The "Dream Team" won gold in Barcelona, Spain. Daly became the first coach to win an NBA championship and an Olympic gold medal.

CHAPTER 3
DETROIT DEFENSE

Chuck Daly left the Pistons in 1992. Isiah Thomas retired from basketball in 1994. The Pistons needed a new star. They found one in swingman **Grant Hill** in 1994. Hill was the co-winner of the Rookie of the Year Award in 1994–95. He was an all-around great player. Hill averaged at least 19 points, six rebounds, and five assists each year on the team.

The Pistons didn't win a lot with Hill, though. Detroit ended up trading him to the Orlando Magic in 2000. One of the players the Pistons got in return was **Ben Wallace**. "Big Ben" was a defensive and rebounding machine. He was the NBA's Defensive Player of the Year four times.

The Pistons added more talent before the 2002–03 season. Detroit drafted **Tayshaun Prince**. The forward annoyed opponents on the defensive end. Prince was named to the All-Defensive Team four times. The Pistons also traded for **Richard "Rip" Hamilton**. The swingman developed into a great three-point shooter. Hamilton led the Pistons in scoring for eight straight seasons.

The Pistons were swept in the conference finals in 2003. Trading for big man

---

STAT SPOTLIGHT

BLOCKS PER GAME IN A SEASON
PISTONS TEAM RECORD
Ben Wallace: 3.5 (2001-02)

Rasheed Wallace in 2004 put the team over the top. "Sheed" had been an offensive star for the Portland Trail Blazers. He sacrificed his scoring numbers in Detroit, though. Wallace dedicated himself to the defensive nature of the Pistons.

Detroit's tough defense led it to an NBA championship. The Pistons defeated the

Los Angeles Lakers in the 2004 NBA Finals. Point guard **Chauncey Billups** was named the Finals Most Valuable Player (MVP). In the Finals, he averaged 21 points and 5.2 assists per game.

After the 2008-09 season, the Pistons began to struggle. That got them plenty of high draft picks. Some young players showed promise. But the losses piled up. The Pistons finally got the top draft pick in 2021. They used it on 6'6" guard **Cade Cunningham**. Detroit fans are hopeful Cunningham can bring another title to the Motor City.

COACH BROWN

Hall of Fame coach Larry Brown made history in 2004. He became the only coach to win championships at both the professional and college levels. He won his college championship in 1988 with the University of Kansas.

TIMELINE

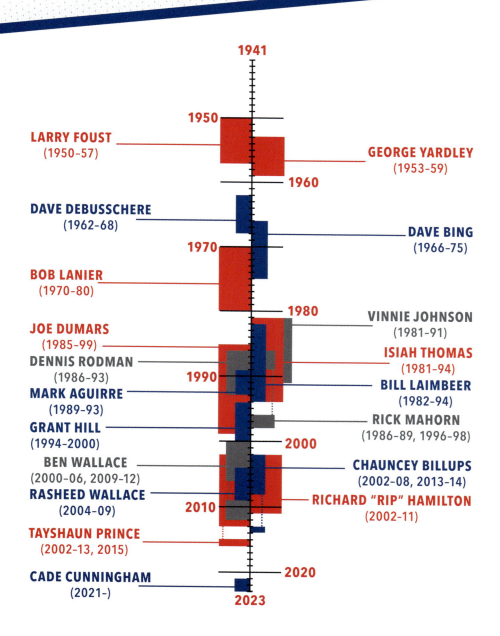

TEAM FACTS

DETROIT PISTONS

Formerly: Fort Wayne Zollner Pistons (1941-42 to 1947-48); Fort Wayne Pistons (1948-49 to 1956-57)

First season: 1941-42

NBA championships: 3*

Key coaches:

Larry Brown (2003-04 to 2004-05)
108-56, 31-17 playoffs, 1 NBA title

Chuck Daly (1983-84 to 1991-92)
467-271, 71-42 playoffs, 2 NBA titles

MORE INFORMATION

To learn more about the Detroit Pistons, go to **pressboxbooks.com/AllAccess**.

These links are routinely monitored and updated to provide the most current information available.

*Through 2021-22 season

GLOSSARY

assists
Passes that lead directly to teammate scoring a basket.

conference
A smaller group of teams that make up part of a sports league.

draft
An event that allows teams to choose new players coming into the league.

enforcer
A tough, physical player who focuses on defense and rebounding.

paint
Another term for the lane, the area between the basket and the free throw line.

rookie
A first-year player.

swingman
A player who can play both guard and forward.

INDEX

Aguirre, Mark, 15

Billups, Chauncey, 21
Bing, Dave, 7, 9
Brown, Larry, 21

Cunningham, Cade, 21

Daly, Chuck, 15, 17
DeBusschere, Dave, 7
Dumars, Joe, 12

Foust, Larry, 5, 7

Hamilton, Richard, 18
Hill, Grant, 17

Johnson, Vinnie, 12

Laimbeer, Bill, 12
Lanier, Bob, 9

Mahorn, Rick, 12

Prince, Tayshaun, 18

Rodman, Dennis, 15

Thomas, Isiah, 11, 17

Wallace, Ben, 17
Wallace, Rasheed, 19

Yardley, George, 5

Zollner, Frank, 7

24